Petrichor
The Divine Scent

Brandon J. J. Board

Book 1 of the Sensory Chronicles
A Poetic Odyssey Through the Five Senses

This is a work of fiction. Names, characters, places, and incidents either are the product of the author's imagination or are used fictitiously. Any resemblance to actual persons, living or dead, events, or locales is entirely coincidental.

Copyright © 2023 by Brandon J. J. Board

All rights reserved. No Part of this book may be reproduced or used in any manner without the written permission of the copyright owner except for the use of quotations in a book review

ISBN:979-8-9888800-1-1(Paperback)
ISBN:979-8-9888800-0-4(Paperback B&W)
ISBN:979-8-9888800-2-8(Ebook)
ISBN:979-8-9888800-3-5(Hardcover)

First Edition: August 2023

Published by StencilFox

Dedication

For Nicole,
My heart, my muse, you're the echo in every word and the rhythm in each verse.

Preface

In my pursuit of exploring the world via the written word, I discovered a unique avenue to illuminate an often-overlooked aspect of life: the human senses. This spark gave birth to "Petrichor - The Divine Scent," the first volume of the "Sensory Chronicles" series.

Why a series? The prospect of creating a connected narrative tapestry, not just a standalone book, was irresistible. The aim was to craft a sensory exploration series that could engage my skills and passion fully.

"Petrichor" is a reflection of this ambition, beginning our sensory voyage with smell due to its intimate link to memory, emotion, and the metaphor of new beginnings.

"Petrichor - The Divine Scent," along with the entire "Sensory Chronicles" series, exists as a testament to pushing boundaries—creating a complex, immersive work that explores the multifaceted human sensory experience. It's my passion project, and I hope it instills in you the same fascination and joy I experienced while crafting it.

Introduction	*14*
Prologue	*16*
Petrichor	*19*
Unstolen Memory	20
Widower's Melody	22
Unending Chase	24
Persistence of Memory	26
Resilience in Raindrops	28
Rainy Reflection	30
Earthbound Oath	32
Piquant	*35*
Spice Journey	36
Stirred Memories	38
Mundane Wisdom	40
Zesty Whims	42
Echoes in the Garden	44
Winter to Spring	46
Symphony of Spice	48
Cloy	*51*
Suffocation to Liberation	52
The Hollowed Toy	54
Cologne of Cunning	56

Fast Food Frenzy	58
Beyond the Smog	60
Unrequited	62
Allure and Ache	64

Sillage — 67

Aromatic Artistry	68
FireSide	70
Relentless Pursuit	72
Scents of Wanderlust	74
Hoodie	76
Echoing Stardust	78
In Their Wake	80

Fetid — 83

Miasma of Malice	84
A Fetid Farting Tale	86
Spiral of Vice	88
Habitual Grip	90
Pungent Persistence	92
Frito Feet	94
Putrid Love	96

Nascent — 99

Birth of Ideas	100

Resilience	102
A Shopaholic Struggle	104
Coffee Beans	106
New Life	108
Invigorating Dew	110
Salt Air and Sea Turtles	112
Redolent	**115**
The Rose of Mary	116
Lilac Love	118
Spiritual Scent	120
Redolent Reminiscences: A Holiday Tale	122
Love's Fragrant Dance	124
Labyrinth of Life	126
Perfumed Chains	128
Afterword	130
Appendix of Poetic Form	132
Bibliography	146
Glossary	148
Acknowledgments	152
About the Author	156

Introduction

Welcome to "Petrichor - The Divine Scent," the first volume of the Sensory Chronicles. This remarkable anthology invites you on a poetic journey through the often overlooked, yet profoundly influential world of olfaction, the sense of smell.

This book is divided into seven captivating sections, each illuminating a unique dimension of scent. Each section is named after a distinctive aroma-related concept— 'Petrichor,' 'Piquant,' 'Cloy,' 'Sillage,' 'Fetid,' 'Nascent,' and 'Redolent.' Within these thematic segments, you will find seven remarkable poems, with each section showcasing a variety of 24 distinct poetic forms.

But worry not, if you are unfamiliar with any of the forms, I have a useful guide in the back of the book. This guide breaks down the structure, origin, and use of each style, providing an educational foundation that will allow you to fully appreciate the depth and artistry of each piece.

And enhancing your experience further, each poem is paired with beautiful artwork, deepening your sensory journey.

I hope that this book impels you to deeply appreciate how our sense of smell and the art of poetry can enrich our understanding of life and relationships. I invite you to immerse yourself in this sensory voyage, and perhaps even carry the scent of petrichor with you, long after you've turned the final page.

Enjoy the journey.

PROLOGUE

In a world where senses are our beacon, a tale begins,
A poetic odyssey, in the language of our skins.
Petrichor, Piquant, Cloy, and Sillage dance,
Fetid, Nascent, Redolent - in this grand expanse.

Petrichor, the earth's sweet sigh, our journey's start,
A divine scent released, a love letter to the heart.
Piquant memories in the air, a spice-laden trail,
Unveiling truths in the mundane, a fragrant gale.

Cloying sweetness, a scent that can bewitch,
Yet, too much, a weight, a veil, a sudden switch.
Sillage, the ghost of a scent, a whispered tale,
A lingering memory, a love that doesn't fail.

Fetid, a warning, a lesson written in the air,
The scent of decay, a reminder to beware.
Nascent, the promise of a scent yet to bloom,
In the wake of creation, the dispelling of gloom.

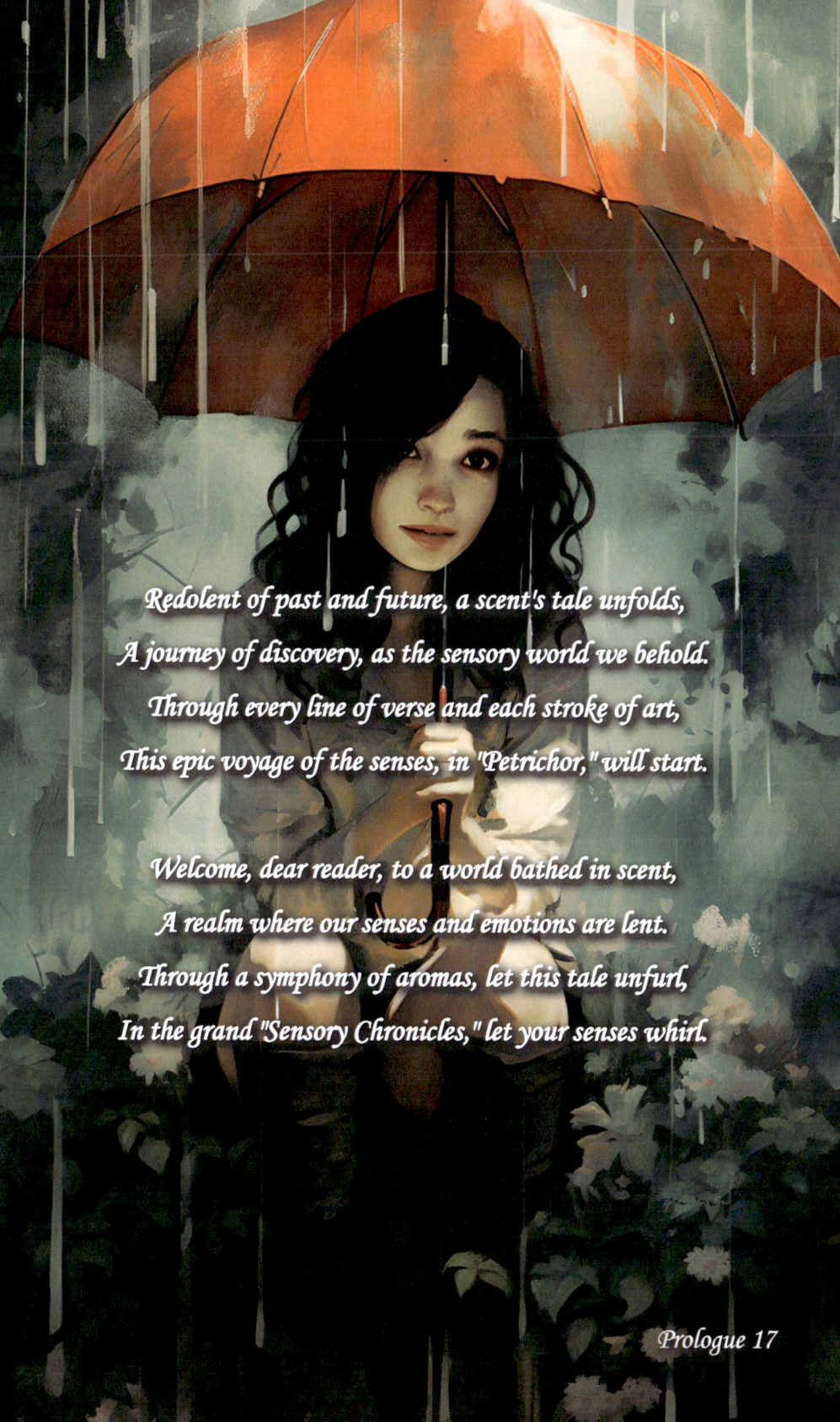

Redolent of past and future, a scent's tale unfolds,
A journey of discovery, as the sensory world we behold.
Through every line of verse and each stroke of art,
This epic voyage of the senses, in "Petrichor," will start.

Welcome, dear reader, to a world bathed in scent,
A realm where our senses and emotions are lent.
Through a symphony of aromas, let this tale unfurl,
In the grand "Sensory Chronicles," let your senses whirl.

Petrichor

```
Petrichor
(peh-tri-kor): noun
```

A pleasant smell that frequently accompanies the first rain after a long period of warm, dry weather.

Ode

UNSTOLEN MEMORY

Ode to the Unstolen Memory

I.

Under the mind's vast dome, a sacred vault,
Housing our memories, where petrichor assaults,
Unscathed by earthly trials, it's our heartfelt waltz,
A timeless dance to the rhythm of life's pulse.

II.

Homes may crumble, jobs may fade,
Families part, and freedoms evade,
Yet, within us, a wealth unswayed,
The scent of memories, ever parades.

III.

Locked in silence, stripped of rights,
In the darkest cell, amid the coldest nights,
Still, the memory ignites,
Petrichor whispers of past delights.

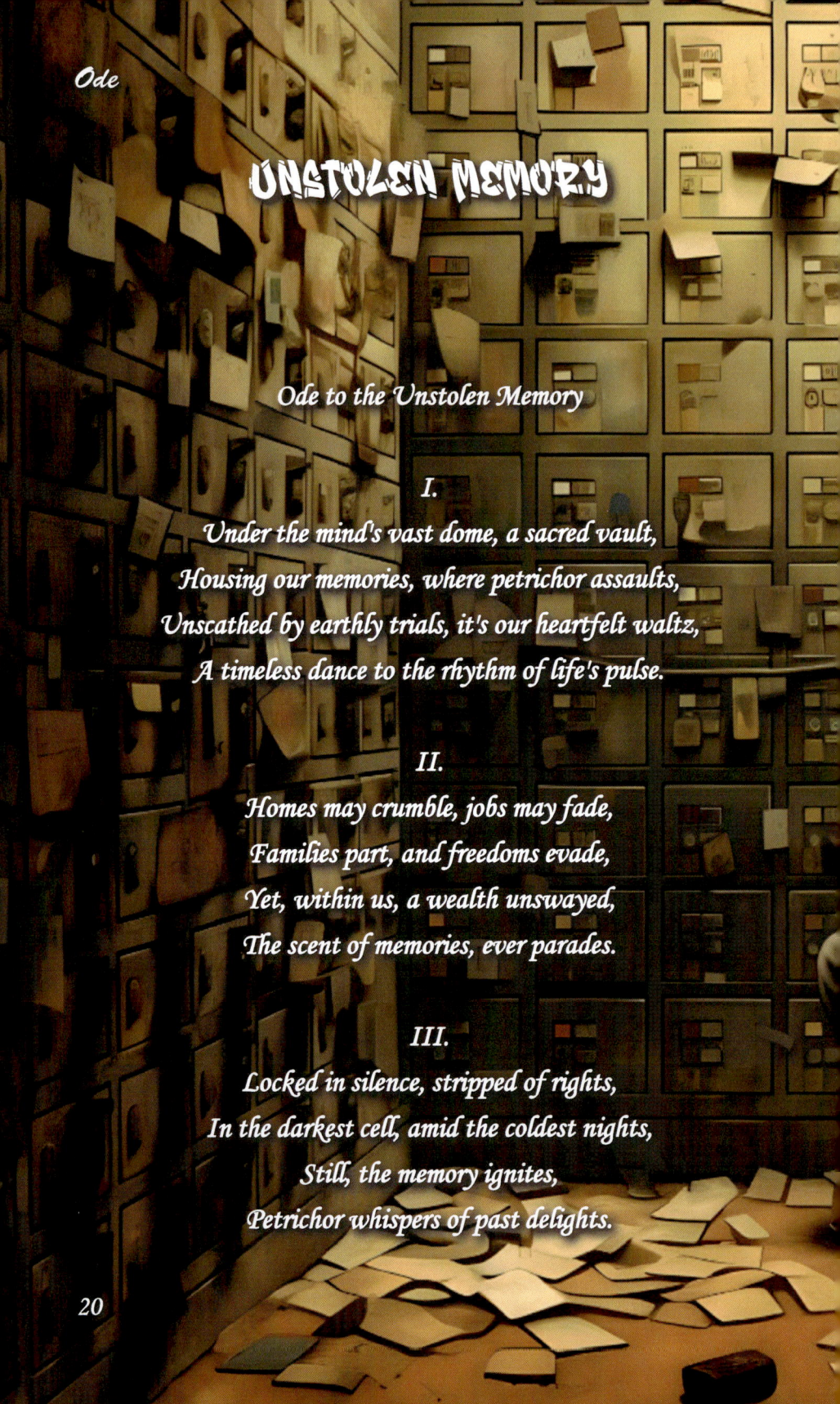

IV.
Invisible threads, finely spun,
Linking moments, one by one,
Petrichor trails where life has run,
Unstolen by time, by man, by none.

V.
Yet, even the strongest minds grow frail,
And memories, like ghosts, grow pale,
The scent of past, a faded trail,
In the labyrinth of mind, they wail.

VI.
Yet, these precious echoes of our past,
In the heart's petrichor, they're vast,
A testament to time, unsurpassed,
In memories, our anchors cast.

VII.
In this dance, time takes its toll,
Yet memories persist, an undying soul.
Yet beware, for even the strongest stronghold
May waver, like twilight's last glowing coal.

Petrichor 21

Limerick

WIDOWER'S MELODY

In a meadow with petrichor's grace,

A widower finds his old place,

With his love's small locket,

In his worn-out pocket,

Memories dance, and he sees her face.

Sonnet

UNENDING CHASE

Love, a harbor amidst life's stormy seas,
Its Petrichor whispers heal, make us whole,
A refuge where weary hearts find their ease,
A sanctuary for the wandering soul.

We're drawn deeper into its soothing calm,
An undercurrent of comfort and care,
In its depths, we discover a healing balm,
A love that enfolds, beyond compare.

Beneath the surface, love's force shapes the sand,
Carving canyons deep within our souls,
With each shared moment, a further land,
Unveiled by the tide's unending rolls.

In love's fathomless depths, we find our grace,
A plunge into eternity, heart's endless chase.

Acrostic

PERSISTENCE OF MEMORY

Petals falling, whispers of the past,
Ephemeral beauty, yet memories last,
Time dances swiftly, yet scents remain,
Rich in remembrance, like petrichor's reign,
Inhaling deeply, the fragrance of days,
Cherishing moments, as time slips away,
Holding to memories, a treasure to savor,
Olfactory echoes, a scent we can favor,
Recalling the past, as present unfurls.

Ars Poetica

Resilience in Raindrops

In the womb of the mind, a poem unfolds,
Petrichor whispers, a tale to be told.
Born from the thoughts, like rain on dry earth,
Poetry's essence, ideas given birth.

Each word that graces the blank, arid page,
An ode to emotion, wisdom, and age.
Ink upon paper, a testament of time,
In petrichor's scent, poetry's rhythm and rhyme.

Through joy and sorrow, love and pain,
Poems mirror the cycle of drought and rain.
In the fleeting moments, both harsh and tender,
Petrichor's aroma makes us remember.

We rise and fall with each poetic dance,
In the theater of words, we take our chance.
Yet, in the heart of struggle, truth persists,
In the scent of petrichor, poetry exists.

When writer's block gathers, do not despair,
For each new idea brings life to the air.
Embrace the tempest, let it quench your soul,
In the scent of petrichor, find inspiration whole.

Poetry's transience, in petrichor's embrace,
A reminder of our place in time and space.
Yet, in its fleeting whisper, an echo of eternity,
The scent of petrichor, poetry's enduring certainty.

Triolet

RAINY REFLECTION

In petrichor's scent, my thoughts take flight,
Through rain-soaked streets, under stars' light,
Unraveling mysteries, both small and grand,
In petrichor's scent, my thoughts take flight.

Where do I stand in this vast expanse?
In the cosmic dance, what is my stance?
In petrichor's scent, my thoughts take flight,
Through rain-soaked streets, under stars' light.

Haibun

EARTHBOUND OATH

In the quiet aftermath of a storm, the world is washed clean, renewed. The scent of petrichor fills the air, earthy and rich, a testament to nature's resilience. It is a scent of promises fulfilled - the rain's promise to the parched earth, the storm's promise of renewal. This fragrance is my constant companion, a reminder of the sacred vows I make.

My word is my bond, a promise as solid as the ground beneath my feet. When I make a vow, it is not just a collection of words, but a solemn commitment. Like the rain that commits to nourishing the earth, I commit to my promises with unwavering dedication. Each pledge I make is a drop of rain, each fulfilled promise a burst of petrichor that permeates my existence.

The world is full of uncertainties, but my word is not one of them. I am steadfast in my commitment, holding myself accountable to the promises I make. I believe that a man is only as good as his word, and I strive to be a man of integrity. The smell of petrichor, a symbol of promises kept, is my guiding principle.

Tasting petrichor,

Promises kept, honor earned,

My word, my essence.

In this world of shifting sands, my promises are my anchors. They ground me, guide me, and define me. And just like the scent of petrichor that follows a storm, the fulfillment of my promises brings a sense of peace and satisfaction that is profound and enduring.

Piquant

Piquant
(pee-kuhnt): adjective

implies a sharp, stinging, or biting quality especially of odors.

Acrostic

SPICE JOURNEY

Piquant aroma, the hot sauce's flair,
Intriguing notes wafting, a fiery affair,
Quintessence of peppers, a spicy delight,
Unique scents mingle, igniting the air right,
Aromatic capsaicin, enticingly rare,
Never stagnant, they rise with dare,
Tantalizing senses, in each breath we share.

Nonet

STIRRED MEMORIES

A piquant scent stirred memories deep,

Echoes of the past began to seep,

Aroma took her to the times,

Of innocence, nursery rhymes,

Nostalgia, a leap,

In memory's keep,

Tears, she weeps,

In sleep,

Steep.

Sestina

MUNDANE WISDOM

In life's weave, there's an art to seeing the unseen,
In the everyday and mundane, we glean,
Subtle truths, like a scent that's always been,
In the air, wisdom speaks in tones serene,
In the humdrum tasks that our lives convene,
Every moment whispers, waiting to convene the scene.

Caught in time's rush, we often set the scene,
With busy minds, ignoring the unseen,
Yet, beneath the bustle, secrets glean,
In every breath, every moment, truths been,
Our lives, though they may seem serene,
Hold fragrant wisdom, like a scent that convenes.

Between lines of the day, subtle and serene,
Lie quiet lessons, waiting to convene,
Beneath the roar, in spaces unseen,
There's an art to seeing, lessons to glean,
In the simplest of acts, wisdom's been,
In life's fragrance, echoes of what's been in the scene.

In the mundane, a tapestry unseen,
In every stitch, every seam, truths convene,
Time, like a river, flows and is serene,
Carrying with it memories of what's been,
To the present moment, observed and glean,
In the scent of life, wisdom convenes the scene.

In the aroma of days, past and glean,
In our hearts, in our souls, love serene,
In the scent of hope, of joy, of the unseen,
We uncover truths, once hidden, been,
In the echoes of the past, in what's serene,
In the everyday and mundane, we convene the scene.

And so, in the quiet that's been the scene,
In the aroma of the morning, we glean,
We discover, in the air, a scent serene,
In the mundane moments, unseen,
There's an art to seeing, a lesson to convene,
In life's fragrance, piquant truths unseen.

In the unseen we convene,
Wisdom's serene, in the glean,
In the echoes of what's been in the scene.

Piquant 41

Limerick

ZESTY WHIMS

A chef with a nose for the rare,
Used spices with utmost care,
A piquant delight,
A smell that took flight,
And filled up the whole market square.

Haibun

ECHOES IN THE GARDEN

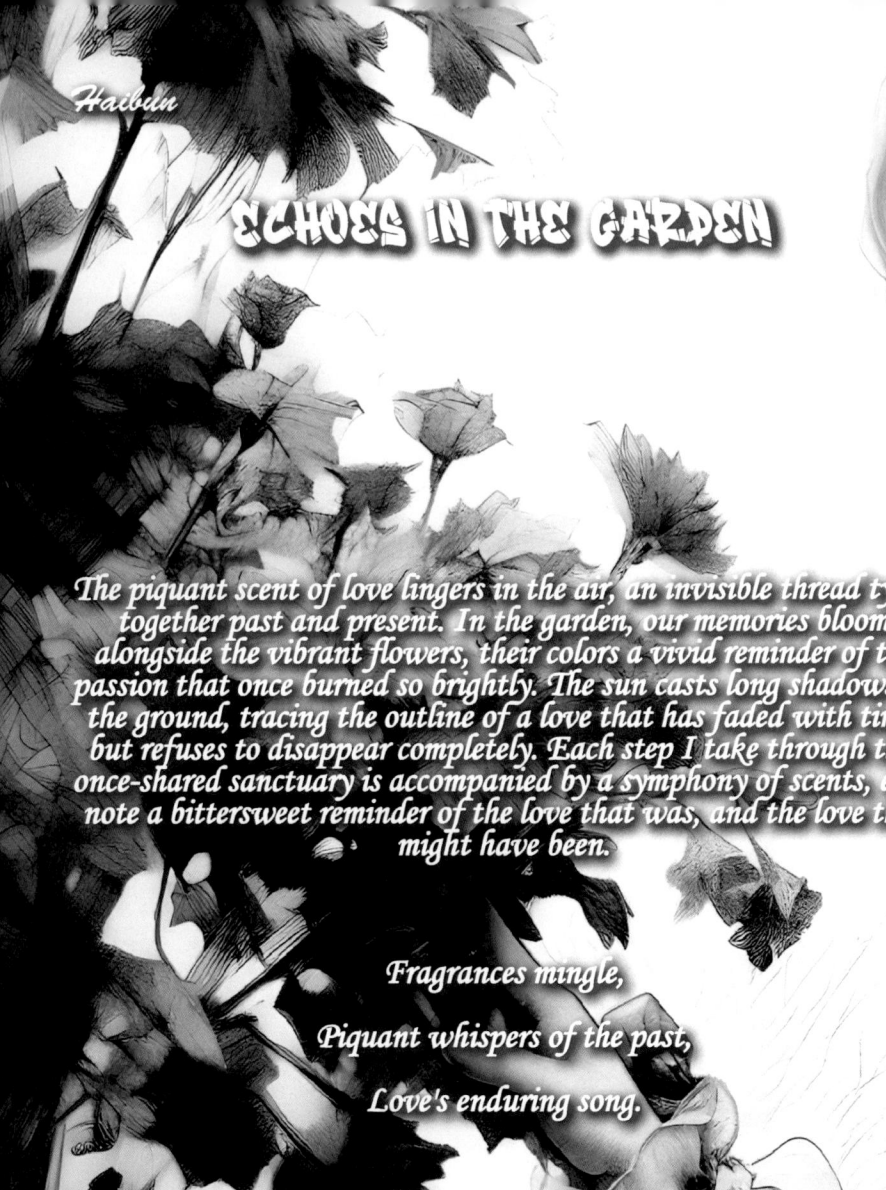

The piquant scent of love lingers in the air, an invisible thread tying together past and present. In the garden, our memories bloom alongside the vibrant flowers, their colors a vivid reminder of the passion that once burned so brightly. The sun casts long shadows on the ground, tracing the outline of a love that has faded with time, but refuses to disappear completely. Each step I take through this once-shared sanctuary is accompanied by a symphony of scents, each note a bittersweet reminder of the love that was, and the love that might have been.

Fragrances mingle,
Piquant whispers of the past,
Love's enduring song.

In the quiet solitude of the garden, I find a sense of peace, a respite from the world outside. The piquant scents of nature offer solace and comfort, reminding me that even in the darkest moments, there is beauty to be found. As I breathe in the rich tapestry of aromas, I am reminded that life, like love, is ever-changing and full of surprises. And as I walk through the garden, the piquant scent of our love lingers, a testament to the power of memory and the indelible mark of a love that will never be forgotten.

Triolet

WINTER TO SPRING

Piquant scents of spring emerge from death,
As winter's icy grip begins to fade,
Life blossoms, inhaling newfound breath,
Piquant scents of spring emerge from death.

Winter's pallor, a memory laid to rest,
As vibrant hues of life in spring cascade,
Piquant scents of spring emerge from death,
As winter's icy grip begins to fade.

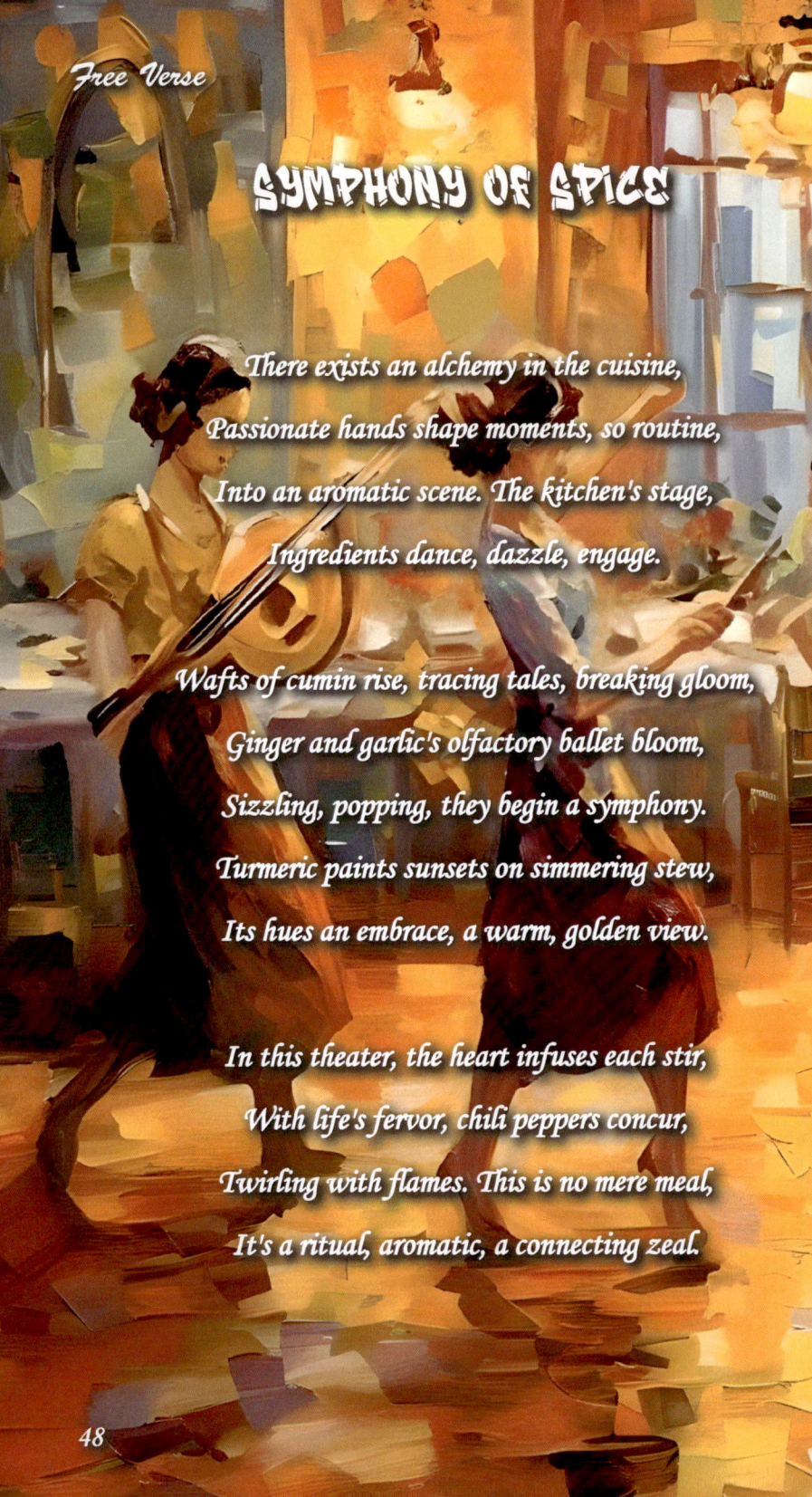

Free Verse

SYMPHONY OF SPICE

There exists an alchemy in the cuisine,
Passionate hands shape moments, so routine,
Into an aromatic scene. The kitchen's stage,
Ingredients dance, dazzle, engage.

Wafts of cumin rise, tracing tales, breaking gloom,
Ginger and garlic's olfactory ballet bloom,
Sizzling, popping, they begin a symphony.
Turmeric paints sunsets on simmering stew,
Its hues an embrace, a warm, golden view.

In this theater, the heart infuses each stir,
With life's fervor, chili peppers concur,
Twirling with flames. This is no mere meal,
It's a ritual, aromatic, a connecting zeal.

Tomatoes, onions join the chorus, deep duet,

Crimson blush, golden tears, in the pan they're met.

Herbs fresh and fragrant, recite green sonnets,

Mingling spices, a poetic procession, savory bonnets.

Flatbreads rest, waiting their turn to play,

With beans and rice, they'll make the palate sway,

A culinary composition now complete,

A feast for senses, flavors, aromas greet.

A plate is set, a dance on the side,

In each bite, a hint of tradition, soul, and pride,

A celebration of life, love, all in between,

A scent of a place, in a kitchen's dream.

Piquant 49

Cloy

Cloy
(kloi): verb

to make weary or cause weariness through an excess of something initially pleasurable or sweet

Slam Poetry

SUFFOCATION TO LIBERATION

Cloying, overwhelming, a memory's haze,
Suffocating sweetness — do you feel it too?
A ghost that won't release, that scent won't leave,
It's you in the air, a phantom's embrace.

You whisper syrupy lies, trapping lies,
Perfume that lingers, a love once treasured,
Now despised, suffocating, a never-ending parade,
But I'll claw out, I'll rise, I'll soar, I'll breathe!

Cloying memories, suffocate no more,
Let me feel the subtler notes of life,
Whispers and secrets that float on the wind,
No longer chained, by your strife.

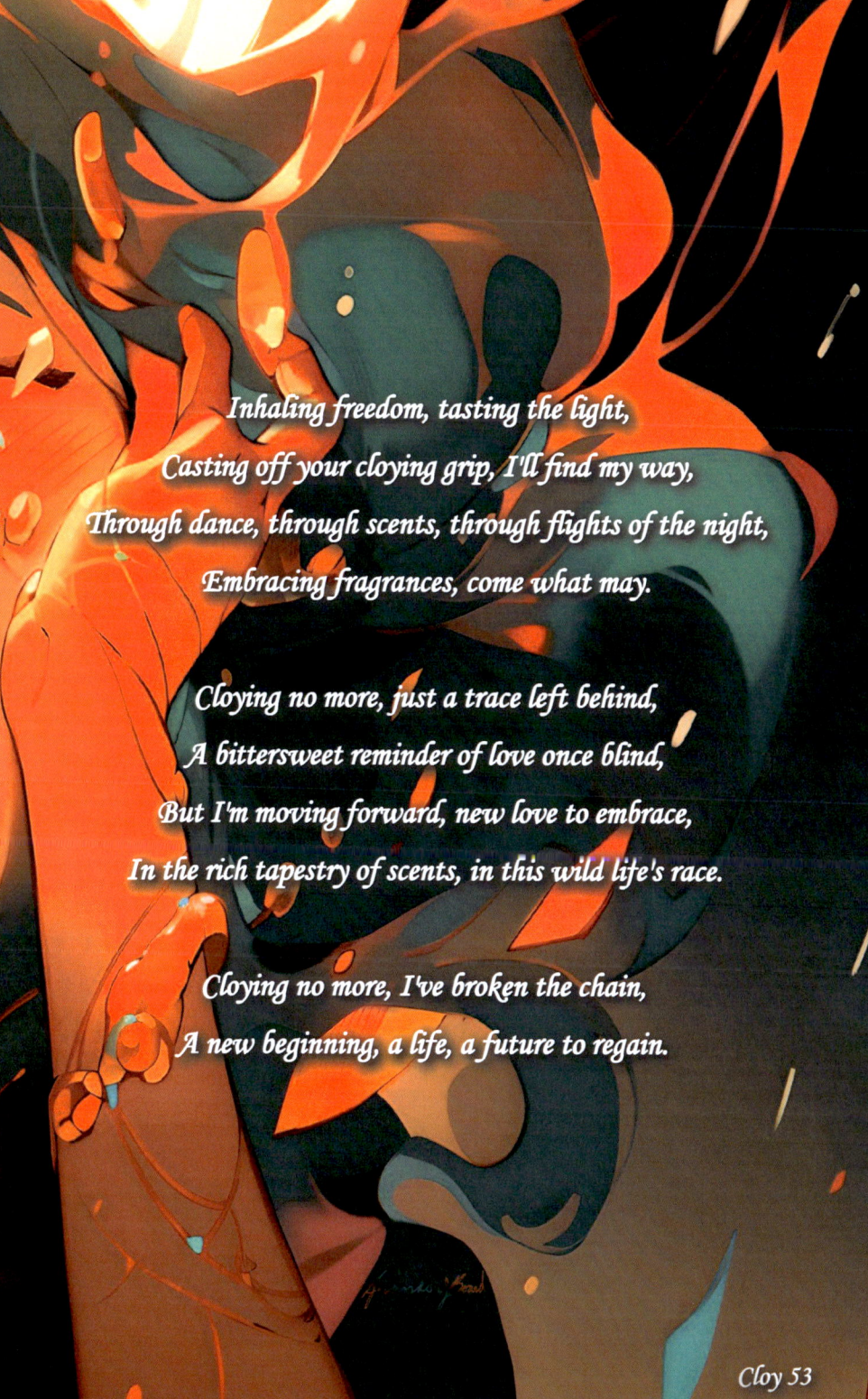

Limerick

THE HOLLOWED TOY

A sweet scent of friendship, a ploy,
Its realness they sought to destroy,
With deceit's odor ripe,
And a trust-breaking swipe,
Their friendship's a hollowed-out toy.

Tautogram

COLOGNE OF CUNNING

Cloying cologne of cunning,
Crafting cover-ups, continually running.
Caught in a cloud of candied deceit,
Cloying cologne of cunning, too sweet.

Concealing corrosion, crafty concealing,
Creating chasms, camaraderie stealing.
Cloying cologne, cunningly creeping,
Canvassing connections, clandestinely seeping.

Causing confusion, candidness culling,
Cloying cologne, cunningly dulling.
Concluding with caution, cohesiveness crumbling,
Cloying cologne of cunning, confounding, humbling

Acrostic

FAST FOOD FRENZY

Cravings for fast food, they never lie,
Lured by the scent of burgers, oh my!
Overwhelmed by fries and shakes piled high,
Yearning for more, with a satisfied sigh!

Sonnet

BEYOND THE SMOG

In the dense, cloying mist of ceaseless brawls,
We strike, then strike once more, losing our track,
In the fleeting time of our mortal crawls,
Divided by wrath, we let our hearts crack.

We grip so firmly to our obstinate ego,
Forgetting we're sailing in this ship together,
In our narrow gaze, we can't perceive the echo,
To a realm of unity, and love's fair weather.

The cloying aroma of malice clouds our sight,
We lose our essence in trivial quarrels,
While the world around us descends into night,
And the melody of peace drowns in the squalls.

Oh, may we find the valor to pierce through the fog,
Beyond the cloying aroma of hate, to the monologue.

Ovillejo

UNREQUITED

Does it leave a mark?

Scar.

Can it douse your spark?

Far.

Is love's journey dark?

Tar.

Scar, far, tar, it's bizarre,
Unrequited love, a lonely star,
In its cloy, emotions spar,
Scar, far, tar, on par,
The stinging reminder, love's bizarre.

Prose

ALLURE AND ACHE

The cloying scent of addiction, sweet and alluring, calls out with a siren's song, drawing in with promises of pleasure, while hiding the pain and darkness that lie beneath. It's a scent that clings to clothes and skin, a constant reminder of the hold that addiction has, a reminder of the way that it poisons the soul and steals away hopes and dreams.

In the shadows of addiction's allure, there's a maze of torment and confusion. It's like wandering through a twisted forest at night, with every path leading further into darkness. The scent becomes a suffocating fog, a trap that entices with ephemeral pleasures but leads only to despair and emptiness. It's a dance with a shadowy partner who leads with a firm grip towards a precipice, a relentless march toward an abyss where dreams wither and hope is but a flicker.

But even as the struggle against its grip continues, drawn back to the scent like a moth to a flame, unable to resist its pull, there is a transformation occurring. There's beauty in the fight against the scent, and in the strive to find the way back to the light, even when darkness threatens to consume.

In the battle against addiction, the struggle itself becomes a beacon of resilience. Like a tree taking root in a barren land, finding nourishment in the cracks of stone, the fight becomes a testament to the human spirit's capacity to endure and overcome. The scent of addiction, once a foul and binding chain, transforms into a reminder of strength and determination, a symbol of a journey not defined by falls, but by rising again.

So let the cloying scent of addiction fill the senses, let it be a reminder of the beauty and the pain, of the struggle and the triumph, of the journey that shapes the soul. It's a path to hope and healing in the face of adversity, a profound lesson that lies within the very heart of human existence.

Sillage

Sillage
(sill-age): noun

the degree to which a perfume's fragrance lingers in the air when worn.

Terza Rima

AROMATIC ARTISTRY

In the realm where discord often breeds,
Sillage of oil paint blooms, a scent unique,
A beacon of hope among the weeds.

Where charcoal's aroma lingers, we seek,
Aromatic tales of the vision and meek,
Words, colors, sounds, the tools to critique.

The sillage of our passion, never bleak,
In its essence, a promise, a mystique,
For in creativity, we find solace unique.

And as every artist reaches their peak,
The fragrance of their craft, a colorful streak,
Of vibrant sillage left by the bold and the chic.

Such is the world where the silent speak,
In the sillage of art, where many critique,
Finds their voice, their strength, even at their weakest.

Unique, in creativity's mystique.

Tanka

FIRESIDE

Night's embrace waning,
Smoky scent in threads remain,
Campfire's sweet refrain.
In my garments, tales reside,
Echoes of a fireside.

Pantoum

RELENTLESS PURSUIT

Setting off on a journey, heart ablaze,
Tearing through life's complex, woven maze,
Seeking answers, in a wild, relentless chase,
Leaving behind a sillage, a vibrant fragrance.

Tearing through life's complex, woven maze,
Every challenge met, no scent left untraced,
Leaving behind a sillage, a vibrant fragrance,
In life's grand theater, we've no role to misplace.

Every challenge met, no scent left untraced,
Learning to move with the world's swift pace,
In life's grand theater, we've no role to misplace,
We sprint, we soar, in this existential race.

Learning to move with the world's swift pace,
Setting off on a journey, heart ablaze,
We sprint, we soar, in this existential race,
Seeking answers, in a wild, relentless chase.

Acrostic

SCENTS OF WANDERLUST

Soothing are the scents that travel brings,
Inhaling the sillage of distant lands,
Longing for the adventure that it sings,
Lured by the whispers of exotic sands,
Aroma of the unknown, excitement it flings,
Guiding our dreams like invisible hands,
Every breath a journey, on memory's wings.

HOODIE

In a hoodie imbued with his grace,
Her heart finds its comforting place,
Sillage whispers love's gentle vow,
A scented embrace she wears now.

With each breath, memories retrace,
His presence, time cannot efface,
A fragrant reminder of home,
In his scent, wherever she'll roam,
Love's silent symbol they embrace,
Their shared bond, time will never erase.

Villanelle

ECHOING STARDUST

We seek our mark in the cosmic sprawl,
A sea of stars, sillage in freefall,
A universe's enigma, inviting us all.

Through the emptiness, we heed the call,
Chasing truths that enthrall,
We seek our mark in the cosmic sprawl.

Countless worlds, time's grand haul,
Galaxies dance in celestial ball,
A universe's enigma, inviting us all.

In starlit hush, we stand tall,
In the vast expanse, we feel small,
We seek our mark in the cosmic sprawl.

Our place in the cosmos, echoing the call,
Through time and space, a sillage scrawl,
We seek our mark in the cosmic sprawl.

A sea of stars, sillage in freefall,
A universe's enigma, inviting us all,
We seek our mark in the cosmic sprawl,
A universe's enigma, inviting us all.

IN THEIR WAKE

Ode to the Sillage of Memories

I.

In quiet moments, when the world stands still,
A tender sillage, subtle, sweet, and mild,
Drifts through the chambers of my heart, until
The memories of mother, father, reconciled.

Oh, how the fragrance lingers, soft and warm,
A whispered touch that stirs the soul to weep,
In the embrace of love, I find a balm,
The sillage of their presence, mine to keep.

II.

The laughter, tears, and lessons they bestowed,
The care and wisdom that they did impart,
In the sillage of their love, forever sowed,
A cherished bond that's etched upon my heart.

For in these fragrant trails, their spirits soar,
A testament of love, forevermore.

III.

As seasons pass, and time may fade away,
Their sillage weaves a tapestry of life,
The joys and sorrows, mingled in the fray,
A symphony of love, through pain and strife.

Oh, sillage of memories, hold me close,
In your embrace, I find the strength to stand,
For in this tender scent, I find repose,
A bridge between two worlds, unseen yet grand.

IV.

Though long since gone, their love shall never wane,
In the sillage of memories, they reside,
For every breath, a glimpse of love's refrain,
A legacy of care, that time defies.

And so, I honor them, with heart held high,
In sillage of their love, that shall not die.

Fetid

Fetid
(fet-id): adjective

having a strong, unpleasant smell; foul-smelling.

Roundel

MIASMA OF MALICE

A fetid stench of malice blooms,
In hearts enwrapped in stifling gloom,
No sweet perfume, but pungent fume,
Malice blooms.

From wounds unseen, the hatred spumes,
A miasma of spite, like a loathsome tomb,
Malice blooms.

To cleanse the air, dispel the doom,
In hearts enwrapped in stifling gloom,
No sweet perfume, but pungent fume,
Malice blooms.

Limerick

A FETID FARTING TALE

There once was a fellow named Bart,
Whose farts were considered an art.
With a fetid release,
A most odorous feast,
He'd make people scatter and dart.

Pantoum

SPIRAL OF VICE

In the grip of vice, we spiral down,
Entwined in chains, fetid as a stagnant lake.
Desire's flame consumes, profound,
Lost in a cycle, for sanity's sake.

Entwined in chains, fetid as a stagnant lake,
We fight the urge, then succumb again.
Lost in a cycle, for sanity's sake,
A never-ending loop of pleasure and pain.

We fight the urge, then succumb again,
As shadows whisper, the scent of deceit teases.
A never-ending loop of pleasure and pain,
Control slips through our fingers with ease.

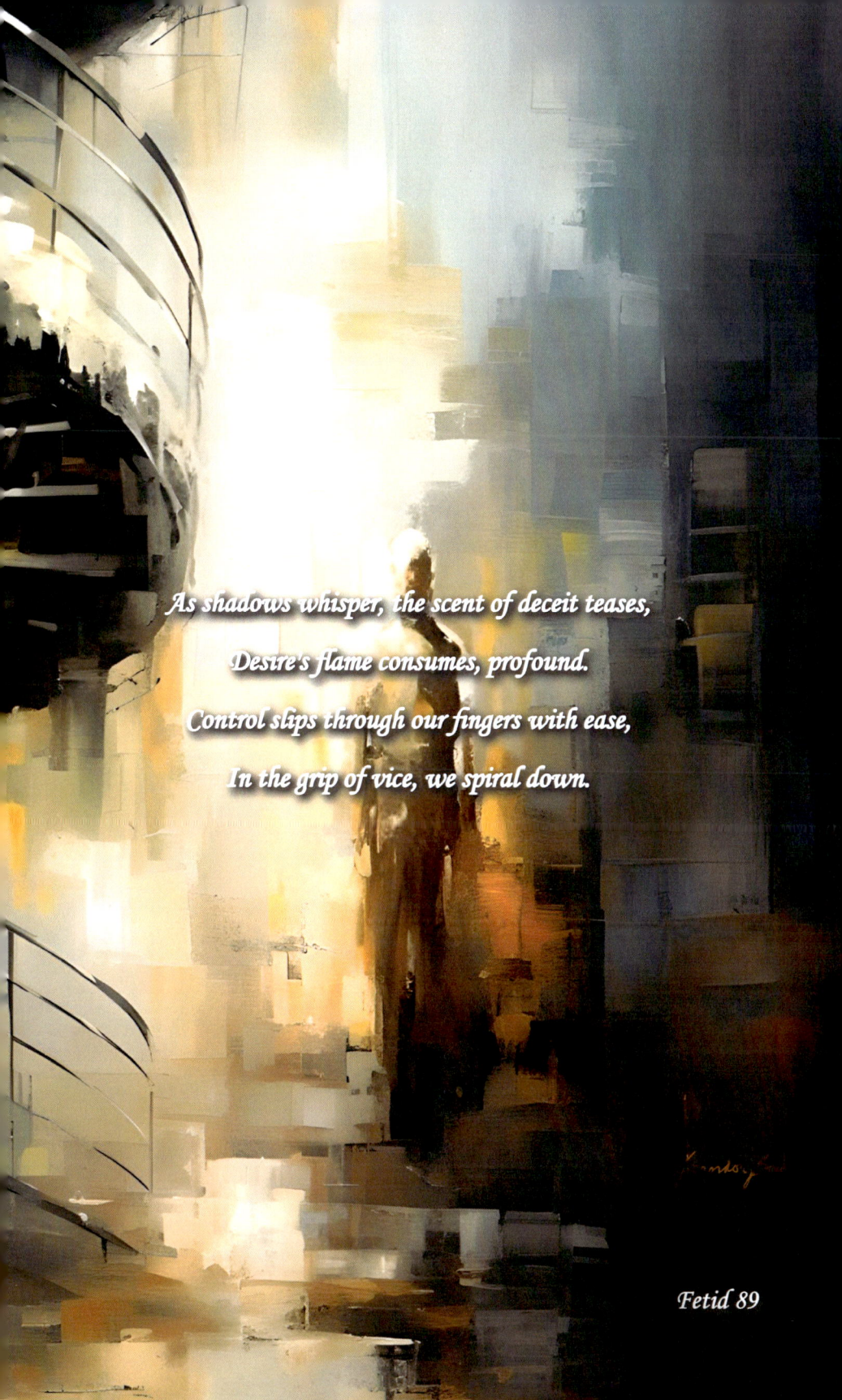

Acrostic

HABITUAL GRIP

Feeding the flames, a fetid ritual,
Ensnared by nicotine's captivating pull.
Tobacco's grip, all too habitual,
Inhaling deeply, the scent of regret, mutual,
Dependency's dance, fetid and brutal.

PUNGENT PERSISTENCE

Upon the crowded gym, the scent does twirl,
A vivid tapestry, stories unfurl,
Each drop of sweat, an unspoken tale,
In harsh exertion's cadence, we unveil.

In sharp tang of perspiration, we find,
The fragrance of battles, left behind,
Musky odor, testament to the fight,
A potent brew, born from strength and might.

Every sinew strains, every heart's ablaze,
Amid the stench of effort, in the maze,
The odor of exertion, raw, unlined,
A pungent testament, power of grind.

Thus, in the gym, strength's scent we hold dear,
Lies beneath the fetid veneer.

Triolet

FRITO FEET

Warm paws hiding a scent so neat,
Bacteria's work, salty, yet sweet.
It's like Fritos beneath doggy feet,
Warm paws hiding a scent so neat.

A strange aroma, yet complete,
In our hearts, it takes a seat.
Warm paws hiding a scent so neat,
Bacteria's work, salty, yet sweet.

PUTRID LOVE

Our love is like a curious concoction, a fetid blend that clings to the senses. It's something that you can almost smell, a mix of repulsion and intoxication, the stench of forbidden fruit. At times, it seems a bouquet of blooming roses, sweet and enticing. But underneath, there's a persistent undercurrent of something more sinister. A whiff of decay, perhaps, or the acrid scent of burnt hopes.

It's our darkest desires, the secrets we wished to keep buried. We find solace in the shadows, comfort in the very things that should repel us. It's intoxicating, suffocating, a heavy aroma that lingers and haunts us. We bathe in it, we consume it, we breathe it in until it fills our very beings, becoming as essential to us as the air we breathe.

We're captives to it, captivated by the scent of longing and despair, helpless, drawn like moths to a fetid flame. It holds us tightly in its grip, pulling us in directions we never intended to go. We sway to its rhythm, helpless to resist, even as we struggle against it, torn between pleasure and guilt, longing and fear.

And we wonder, in the musky fragrance of this dark enchantment, is it possible to break free from its spell? Can we get out of this intoxicating concoction that has so thoroughly ensnared us? The solution eludes us, always just out of grasp, like the enticing aroma of a faraway perfume, vexing in its subtlety.

As we grapple with these questions, the intoxication deepens, the desire strengthens. We know that this twisted love, this enthralling aroma, may be our ruin. And yet, we cannot turn away. We get lost in it, enthralled by its complexity and entangled by its various layers. We enjoy exploring its depths even as we fear what we might discover.

In the end, perhaps it is this very uncertainty, this mingling of pleasure and pain, attraction and revulsion, that defines us, that makes this strange, unnameable thing we share so uniquely ours. It's a love like no other, an addiction, a poison, a balm. It's a paradox, a mystery, a riddle without an answer. It's a scent we'll always carry with us, a fragrance that defines us, a love we'll never forget or fully comprehend.

Nascent

Nascent
(nas-uhnt): adjective

a budding or developing stage, especially of a smell or taste.

Tautogram

BIRTH OF IDEAS

Nascent notions nurtured, now necessary,
Navigating neural networks, nimbly, no adversary.
Never negating, newly networking,
Nascent neurons nimbly nestling.

Limerick

RESILIENCE

There once was a sapling so wee,
In shadows, it struggled to be,
But with care and with time,
It commenced its slow climb,
Nascent growth, overcoming with glee.

Haibun

A SHOPAHOLIC STRUGGLE

In the dim light of dawn, I set out on a familiar journey, drawn by an inexplicable compulsion. The quiet of the early morning offers a stark contrast to the frenzy that awaits me. I am both a traveler and a captive, bound by an unspoken pact with my yearning. A sense of anticipation takes root, nascent like the first whispers of morning.

I wander through the glossy maze of aisles, each display more enticing than the last. The rustle of shopping bags in my grasp serves as a rhythmic chorus to my aimless pilgrimage. Each acquisition feels like a triumph - a temporary panacea for an unending quest.

Yet, the luster of this hollow victory fades as swiftly as it comes. It's an ephemeral high, quickly drowned by the tidal wave of guilt and regret. The void within refuses to be filled, the gnawing hunger remains unappeased. I look upon my bounty, a stark reminder of my indulgence, and I am overcome with despair.

I retreat into the silent solace of my refuge, surrounded by my acquisitions - each object a testament to my insatiable thirst. I am trapped in a cycle of yearning and remorse. Yet, the promise of a new dawn brings with it the nascent hope of redemption - an opportunity to break free from my shackles.

Harsh light unveils harsh truths,

In empty halls echo spent laughter,

Silent cries of insatiable wants.

Acrostic

COFFEE BEANS

Nestled in the bag, a promise so sweet,
Aroma of coffee beans, a delightful treat.
Shadows of the morning, the scent does beat,
Coffee's magic, in every heartbeat.
Every bean, a journey so fleet,
Nascent aroma, subtly replete,
Through the scent, the morning we greet.

Villanelle

NEW LIFE

In my arms, a miracle takes form,

The nascent scent of a newborn so sweet,

A lullaby, in the quiet of the morn.

Soft coos and gurgles, a symphony born,

In your eyes, I see life's tale complete,

In my arms, a miracle takes form.

Tiny fingers wrapped around, adorn,

A moment's sillage, fleeting yet replete,

A lullaby, in the quiet of the morn.

In your breath, a love that's yet unsworn,

A new dawn, as heartbeats synchronously beat,

In my arms, a miracle takes form.

As you grow, may you never mourn,

The nascent scent of innocence discrete,

A lullaby, in the quiet of the morn.

In this scent, a promise not forlorn,

A journey begins, as our lives meet,

In my arms, a miracle takes form,

A lullaby, in the quiet of the morn.

Nascent 109

INVIGORATING DEW

Nascent morning's glow,

Scent of dew,

Daybreak's pure delight.

Epic

SALT AIR AND SEA TURTLES

Prologue: The Sea's Eternal Song

In the realm where sky meets ocean's embrace,
Where dreams take flight and time leaves no trace,
A prophecy whispered on salted breeze,
Foretold a hero born of the seas.

A turtle of both current and tide,
Destined to roam, no land to abide,
In the heart of the ocean, a quest unfolds,
A tale of courage, wisdom, and ages old.

Part I: The Nascent Morn

In the heart of the nascent morn, ere the sun has kissed the sea,
Rises the scent of the salt air, the breath of the ocean, free.
It sweeps across the white-capped waves, dancing with the breeze,
A scent as old as time itself, carried with such ease.

That salty tang, a tale it tells, of the ocean's vast expanse,
Of mysteries that lay beneath, in a haunting, timeless dance.
From shore to shore, the call rings true, a love song to the deep,
Where ancient creatures stir below, their secrets yet to keep.

Part II: The Birth of a Hero

In a hidden cove where waters embrace the land,
A turtle was hatched, a destiny so grand.
The sea's song marked its birth, a sacred melody from yore,
Guided by the salt air's scent, it reached the ocean floor.

The creatures of the sea sensed the hero's solemn dance,
Saw in the turtle a glimmer, a mystic ocean's trance.
Through trials and triumphs, it would grow, the waves its guide so clear,
In the briny perfume of the deep, its path would soon appear.

Part III: The Journey's Challenge

The hero, the turtle, a path did pursue,
Through currents and tempests, it ever knew,
A destiny waiting beyond the horizon,
Guided by love of the sea, the path chosen.

Through coral reefs, vibrant, where secrets reside,
Past shadows lurking, nowhere to hide,
The turtle faced trials, a test of the heart,
Each struggle and battle, wisdom to impart.

In this dance of life, challenges faced,
Lessons learned, and fears embraced,
A bond with the sea, unbreakable, strong,
In its waves and its depths, the turtle belonged.

Part IV: The Whisper of Legends

A legend was whispered, an ancient tale,
Of a treasure hidden, beyond storm and gale,
A power to heal, unite, and restore,
The ocean's balance, its beauty to implore.

The turtle, the hero, sensed a quest untold,
A journey toward mysteries, a destiny foretold.
With allies and guides, the sea's noble creatures,
It followed the whispers, the ocean's wise teachers.

Through caverns and abyss, the path wound,
Each twist and turn, a truth newfound,
The love of the sea's salt air, a beacon, a guide,
In the dance of waves, no secrets could hide.

The epic grows, a saga of sea,
A tale of a turtle, brave and free,
A story to be told, through ages and time,
In the heart of the ocean, a love so sublime.

To be continued...

Nascent 113

Redolent

```
         Redolent
   (red-l-uhnt): adjective
```

having a strong, pleasant odor.

Ovillejo

THE ROSE OF MARY

Is it the scent of joy?

Pure.

Does it love deploy?

Sure.

Can it ever cloy?

Lure.

Pure, sure, lure, the allure,

Redolent rosemary, I adore,

In its aroma, euphoria we explore,

Pure, sure, lure, encore,

The herb's scent, I implore.

Redolent 117

Ode

LILAC LOVE

Ode to the Lilac Love:

I.

In gardens of the heart where love resides,
Among the blooming roses, jasmines white,
There stands a lilac, blooming in my strides,
Your essence, love, a redolent delight.

II.

The petals, soft as whispers in the night,
Are mirrored in your tender, caring touch,
Their color, like the dusk's gentle twilight,
Reflects the depth of love I hold so much.

III.

Their fragrance, sweet, intoxicating, pure,
Like melodies that play when you're near,
Fills the air, creating an allure,
In your presence, love, I've nothing to fear.

IV.

In your nurturing light, our shared love soars,
Your essence feeds my heart, it forever implores,
The sun to my lilac, the core to my spores,
In your glow, our boundless love explores.

V.

In lilac's bloom, I see your soul's embrace,
In each petal, a testament of grace,
Our lives entwined, a never-ending dance,
In the garden of love, a perfect romance.

VI.

So here, my love, in words, your essence etched,
A lilac's tale, our love story sketched,
Your love, a lilac in my heart's soft clutch,
A love so profound, it equals such.

Roundel

SPIRITUAL SCENT

Copal's redolent aroma in the air,
An offering to gods, in reverence and care,
Tales of old, in fragrant wisps, relate,
Aroma in the air.

In sacred rituals, its scent is shared,
In silent prayer, the mortal and divine pair,
Aroma in the air.

In copal's scent, a story lies bare,
Of an ancient people, their traditions declare,
Tales of old, in fragrant wisps, relate,
Aroma in the air.

Acrostic

REDOLENT REMINISCENCES: A HOLIDAY TALE

Reveling in warmth, a home adorned,
Evergreen scent fills the room, forlorn,
Dancing flames crackle, cast shadows that twist,
Olfactory delight of cookies, hard to resist.
Lingering aroma of mulled wine, so sweet,
Embrace of nostalgia, as past and present meet,
Nostalgic whispers of cinnamon and pine,
Tales of Holiday's past, in every scent, align.

Sonnet

LOVE'S FRAGRANT DANCE

In sweet embrace, a love so tender,
Upon thy neck, a scent does linger,
With every breath, the scent grows deeper,
Love's aroma, a constant keeper,

Redolent whispers, soft surrender,
Entwined, our hearts become a singer,
Through love's tempest, we are the reaper,
In fragrance lies a love that's steeper,

As petals fall and blossoms wither,
Love's perfume shall never slither,
Forever strong, a bond to tether,
In redolent notes, we'll dance together,

For in love's scent, a memory stays,
A redolent dance, through endless days.

Villanelle

LABYRINTH OF LIFE

In life's grand maze, a labyrinth we tread,
Redolent of danger, steeped in dread,
Each twist and turn, a choice to make, a line to thread.

No map to guide, no star to light our head,
Only instinct and hope, on which we're fed,
In life's grand maze, a labyrinth we tread.

Echoing footsteps haunt the path we've led,
The scent of fear, a scent that's widely spread,
Each twist and turn, a choice to make, a line to thread.

In shadows lurk the doubts and fears we've fled,
Our past mistakes, reminders of the dead,
In life's grand maze, a labyrinth we tread.

Yet, courage stirs, a flame that's fiery red,
In heart's resolve, we find our homestead,
Each twist and turn, a choice to make, a line to thread.

For in the labyrinth, life's truths are said,
To find our way, by our own hand we're led,
In life's grand maze, a labyrinth we tread,
Each twist and turn, a choice to make, a line to thread.

Redolent 127

PERFUMED CHAINS

Redolent hints,

Fragrance calls,

Addicts me.

Inhale deep,

Caught in dance,

Can't escape.

Yearning grows,

Never filled,

Craving more.

Afterword

As we conclude this introductory journey, I find it important to acknowledge that change is the only constant, and indeed, the same philosophy holds true for this series. The structure of "Petrichor - The Divine Scent" has been carefully crafted to take you on a specific sensory voyage, but as we continue our journey through the "Sensory Chronicles," expect the unexpected.

I believe in embracing the diversity and richness of the human sensory experience, and to reflect this, the structure of future volumes may shift and evolve. Staying static is not in my nature, nor is it reflective of the ever-changing world we perceive through our senses. It is my promise to you that while each book will undoubtedly be a sensory exploration, no two will be the same in structure or approach.

So, as we journey onward, be prepared for change, embrace it, and relish the exciting unpredictability of this sensory odyssey. After all, it's the variations in our experiences that make them truly worth cherishing.

Appendix of Poetic Form

Dear reader,

As you journey through the pages of this book, you'll find yourself immersed in a world shaped by a rich variety of poetic forms. Each poem's structure isn't just a random choice; it's a deliberate decision that shapes the rhythm, flow, and feel of the words. Understanding these forms can add a whole new layer to your reading experience, unveiling the careful craftsmanship behind each line and stanza.

This appendix serves as your personal guide to the poetic forms used throughout the book. For each form, you'll find a brief history, a description of its structure, and a few fun facts. Whether you're a seasoned poetry lover or new to the world of verse, this guide can offer fresh insights and deepen your appreciation of the art.

Feel free to use this appendix in a way that enhances your journey. You may want to refer to it as you read each poem, explore it in full after you've read the book, or even dive into it now to get a taste of what's to come. The choice is entirely yours.

May these insights into poetic forms add another dimension to your reading journey, illuminating the intricate artistry behind each word, line, and stanza."

With warm regards,
Brandon J. J. Board

INTRODUCTION TO RHYME SCHEMES

Understanding a poem's rhyme scheme can greatly enhance your appreciation of the structure and intricacies of the verse. A rhyme scheme is the pattern of end rhymes or lines in a poem, typically denoted by the use of different letters for each new rhyme.

Let's explore this concept using one of the most classic forms of poetry: the sonnet. Specifically, we'll consider the Shakespearean sonnet, which follows a rhyme scheme of ABABCDCDEFEFGG.

Shakespear's Sonnet 18

Shall I compare thee to a summer's day? (A)
Thou art more lovely and more temperate: (B)
Rough winds do shake the darling buds of May, (A)
And summer's lease hath all too short a date: (B)

Sometime too hot the eye of heaven shines, (C)
And often is his gold complexion dimmed, (D)
And every fair from fair sometime declines, (C)
By chance, or nature's changing course, untrimmed: (D)

But thy eternal summer shall not fade (E)
Nor lose possession of that fair thou ow'st; (F)
Nor shall Death brag thou wander'st in his shade, (E)
When in eternal lines to time thou grow'st: (F)

So long as men can breathe or eyes can see, (G)
So long lives this, and this gives life to thee. (G)

Upon closer observation, you'll notice that this sonnet is divided into three quatrains (four-line stanzas) and a final couplet (two-line stanza). Each section is marked by shifts in the rhyme scheme, contributing to the progression of the poem's argument.

In more complex forms of poetry, the rhyme scheme can become increasingly nuanced and intertwined with the poem's meaning, revealing a beautiful symmetry between form and content. As you delve into the various styles of poetry featured in this anthology, take a moment to appreciate the unique rhyme schemes and how they contribute to the overall effect of each poem.

ACROSTIC

Origins and History:
The term Acrostic comes from the French 'acrostiche,' derived from post-classical Latin 'acrostichis,' which itself originates from the Ancient Greek words 'ἄκρος' (meaning 'highest, topmost') and 'στίχος' (meaning 'verse').

Structure:
An Acrostic is a form of writing where the first letter, syllable, or word of each line or paragraph spells out a word, message, or the alphabet when read vertically. The length can vary depending on the word or phrase being spelled out.

Notable Works and Creators:
Acrostics have been used for centuries across multiple cultures and languages. They do not have a single creator or period of fame. However, one famous example of an Acrostic is the first-century Latin Sator Square.

Unique Features:
Acrostics can be used in poetry and prose and can be about any subject. They are often used as a mnemonic device to aid memory retrieval. The key feature of an Acrostic is the hidden word or message that is revealed when the first letter (or syllable, or word) of each line or paragraph is read vertically from top to bottom. Variations include the telestich, where the last letter of each line forms a word, and the double acrostic, which combines both an acrostic and a telestich.

ARS POETICA

Origins and History:
The term "Ars Poetica" comes from Latin and translates to "The Art of Poetry." It was first used as the title of a poem by the Roman poet Horace in 19 BC, who set forth his principles of poetry in it.

Structure:
Unlike many other forms of poetry, Ars Poetica does not have a strict meter, rhyme, or stanza structure. Instead, it is characterized by its content rather than its form. An Ars Poetica poem is a reflection or meditation on the art of poetry itself, either as a general concept or the poet's personal philosophy on poetry. It is essentially a poem about poetry.

Notable Works and Creators:
Several notable poets have penned their own versions of Ars Poetica, including Archibald MacLeish, whose succinct Ars Poetica famously declares, "A poem should not mean / But be." Ezra Pound and Alexander Pope have also written influential poems in this style.

Unique Features:
What sets Ars Poetica apart is its subject matter. It is a metapoetic form that encourages poets to step back and consider their craft at a broader level. Poems in this style are introspective and philosophical, often grappling with questions about the purpose, nature, and value of poetry itself.

EPIC

Origins and History:
The epic is one of the earliest poetic forms, with roots in ancient oral traditions. Epics are long, narrative poems that recount the deeds and adventures of heroic or legendary figures. Ancient epics, such as the Iliad and the Odyssey, were originally recited orally and later written down.

Structure:
Epic poems are characterized by their length and often consist of several books or sections. They typically employ a formal diction and are written in elevated language. Most epics contain elements such as a hero of national significance, a vast setting, supernatural forces, and a central heroic quest or mission.

Notable Works and Creators:
Some of the most renowned epics include Homer's Iliad and Odyssey, Virgil's Aeneid, and John Milton's Paradise Lost. More recent epics include Derek Walcott's Omeros and Ezra Pound's Cantos.

Unique Features:
Epics often begin in medias res (in the middle of things) and utilize features like epic similes, epithets, and invocations to the muse. They typically aim to convey the cultural values and history of a people.

ESPINELA

Origins and History:
Espinela, also known as décima, is a poetic form that originated in Spain in the 16th century. It is named after its creator, Vicente Espinel, a Spanish writer and musician.

Structure:
The espinela consists of ten lines, typically octosyllabic (eight syllables per line), and has a rhyme scheme of ABBAACCDDC. The poem can be written on any subject and can be either serious or humorous.

Notable Works and Creators:
Vicente Espinel is the creator of this form and wrote many espinelas. The form later spread to Latin America and became popular in various musical genres, especially in improvised verse singing contests.

Unique Features:
The espinela is known for its intricate rhyme scheme and is often used in musical compositions, particularly in Latin America. It is also a popular form for improvisational poetry competitions where poets must create espinelas on the spot based on given themes.

FREE VERSE

Origins and History:
Free verse is a modernist poetic form that emerged in the late 19th and early 20th centuries as poets began to break away from traditional poetic structures.

It was popularized by poets such as Walt Whitman and Ezra Pound.

Structure:
Free verse poems do not conform to any specific meter, rhyme scheme, or structure. They allow poets complete freedom in terms of line breaks, rhythm, and form, and often closely follow natural speech patterns.

Notable Works and Creators:
Walt Whitman's "Leaves of Grass" is considered one of the most influential collections of free verse poetry. Other notable poets who have written in free verse include T.S. Eliot, Ezra Pound, and Allen Ginsberg.

Unique Features:
The defining feature of free verse is its lack of formal structure. Poets are free to experiment with line lengths, enjambment, punctuation, and other poetic devices to create a unique voice and style.

HAIBUN

Origins and History:
Haibun is a Japanese literary form that combines prose with haiku. It was developed in the 17th century and was popularized by the Japanese poet Matsuo Basho.

Structure:
A Haibun typically begins with a paragraph or more of prose, followed by a haiku. The prose is usually descriptive, and the haiku serves to deepen the imagery or feeling of the prose.

Notable Works and Creators:
Matsuo Basho is perhaps the most famous haibun writer, and his work "Oku no Hosomichi" (The Narrow Road to the Deep North) is considered a masterpiece of the form.

Unique Features:
What sets haibun apart is the combination of prose and haiku, where the haiku enhances the themes and imagery of the prose, often creating a contrast or deepening the emotion.

HAIKU

Origins and History:
Haiku is a traditional form of Japanese poetry that dates back to the 17th century. It evolved from the earlier hokku and was popularized by poets such as Matsuo Basho, Yosa Buson, and Kobayashi Issa.

Structure:
Traditional haiku consists of three lines with a syllabic pattern of 5-7-5. It often focuses on images from nature and includes a seasonal word (kigo) and a cutting word (kireji) that serves as a kind of punctuation.

Notable Works and Creators:
Matsuo Basho is considered one of the greatest haikupoets, and his poem "An

old silent pond..." is one of the most famous haikus ever written.

Unique Features:
Haiku often captures a moment in time, and its brevity is aimed at evoking emotions and imagery in a very concise form. It traditionally includes a focus on nature and seasons.

LIMERICK

Origins and History:
The limerick is a form of poetry that has its origins in Ireland and gained popularity in English literature in the 19th century. Edward Lear, a British author and poet, is largely responsible for popularizing the form.

Structure:
A limerick is a five-line poem, predominantly anapestic trimeter, with a strict rhyme scheme of AABBA. The first, second, and fifth lines rhyme, while the third and fourth lines are shorter and share a different rhyme.

Notable Works and Creators:
Edward Lear's "Book of Nonsense" (1846) is one of the most famous collections of limericks.

Unique Features:
The first line of a limerick traditionally introduces a person and a place. Limericks are known for their humor, often involving word play and puns, and sometimes have a nonsensical or absurd theme

LUNE

Origins and History:
The Lune is also known as the American Haiku and was created by the American poet Robert Kelly as a response to his frustration with English haikus. The Lune is a 13-syllable, self-contained poem. There is also a variant of Lune created by Jack Collom.

Structure:
There are two variants of the Lune. The original form created by Robert Kelly consists of 13 syllables distributed over three lines in a 5/3/5 syllable pattern. The variant created by Jack Collom is word-based and consists of three lines with a 3/5/3 word pattern.

Notable Works and Creators:
Robert Kelly, a renowned poet, created the Lune. Jack Collom later introduced a word-based variant of the form.

Unique Features:
The Lune is often used to capture a single moment or image in a concise form. It is similar to the Haiku but adapted to the English language. The Lune's primary feature is its three-line structure with a fixed syllable or word count. It's a form that captures brevity similar to the traditional Japanese Haiku.

NONET

Origins and History:
The Nonet is a relatively modern form of poetry and does not have a specific cultural or geographic origin.

Structure:
A Nonet consists of nine lines. The first line has nine syllables, the second line has eight syllables, the third line has seven syllables, and so on, until the ninth line, which has just one syllable. The total syllable count of a Nonet is 45. Rhyming is optional.

Notable Works and Creators:
The creator of the Nonet form is unknown. However, this form has gained some popularity in contemporary poetry for its simple yet challenging structure.

Unique Features:
Nonets can cover any subject matter. Because of their decreasing structure, they're often used to illustrate themes of decline, loss, or diminishing. Alternatively, they can also represent a journey to the essential or the core of a subject. The key feature of the Nonet is its syllable pattern, which decreases with each line. This gives the poem a unique visual shape, often resembling a funnel or an inverted pyramid. The Nonet's structure encourages conciseness and precision in word choice.

ODE

Origins and History:
The ode is an ancient poetic form that originated in Ancient Greece. It was used for formal poetry on various subjects, including love, mourning, and praise. Famous Greek poets who wrote odes include Pindar and Horace.

Structure:
An ode is typically a long, elaborate poem with a formal structure. It is characterized by its elevated style, complex stanza forms, and use of varied meters. It often praises or glorifies an event, individual, or object.

Notable Works and Creators:
John Keats is known for his odes, such as "Ode on a Grecian Urn," "Ode to a Nightingale," and "To Autumn." Other notable poets who have written odes include Percy Bysshe Shelley and William Wordsworth.

Unique Features:
Odes are known for their formal and elevated language, elaborate structure, and emotional intensity. They often involve intricate patterns of stanzas and meter, and typically celebrate or praise their subjects.

OVILLEJO

Origins and History:
The Ovillejo is an old Spanish poetic form, which dates back to the 16th century. The name "ovillejo" translates to "small ball of thread" in English, a metaphorical reference to the way the poem wraps up in its final lines.

Structure:

The Ovillejo is composed of 10 lines with a specific syllable count and rhyme scheme. The first six lines are made up of octosyllabic and hexasyllabic lines, followed by a redondilla quatrain. The rhyme scheme is aabbbaabcC, where the capital 'C' represents the final line that combines lines 'a', 'b', and 'c' in a summarizing statement. The syllable count for each line follows the pattern: 8, 4, 8, 4, 8, 4, 8, 4, 8, 10.

Notable Works and Creators:
The Ovillejo was not invented by a specific poet, but rather evolved as a form in Spanish literature. The form is often associated with Miguel de Cervantes, who popularized the Ovillejo in his work "Don Quixote". Cervantes used the form to convey complex thoughts and ideas with brevity and precision.

Unique Features:
The Ovillejo is known for its tight structure and clever wordplay. The repeating lines allow for themes to be developed and then cleverly tied together in the final line. This form is excellent for exploring a single idea or image in depth.

PANTOUM

Origins and History:
The pantoum is a poetic form that originated in Malaysia, adopted by French poets in the 19th century. It is derived from the Malayan pantun, a traditional oral form of expression. The pantoum was later adopted by various Western poets, including Charles Baudelaire and Victor Hugo.

Structure:
A pantoum consists of a series of quatrains (4-line stanzas) and employs a series of repeated lines. The rhyme scheme is ABAB in each quatrain. The second and fourth lines of each quatrain are repeated as the first and third lines of the next quatrain. The final stanza repeats the second and fourth lines of the penultimate stanza as its first and third lines and uses the first and third lines of the first stanza as its second and fourth lines.

Notable Works and Creators:
Charles Baudelaire's "Harmonie du Soir" is an example of a pantoum in French. In English, the form has been used by poets such as Donald Justice and John Ashbery.

Unique Features:
The pantoum is characterized by its use of repeated lines and a specific rhyme scheme, creating a circular and interwoven structure. It often has a musical quality due to the repeated lines.

PROSE POETRY

Origins and History:
Prose poetry originated in 19th-century France as a reaction to the constraints of traditional verse forms. It emerged as a literary form that combines the characteristics of prose and poetry and is associated with the Romantic and Symbolist movements.

Structure:
Prose poetry is written in prose format, without line breaks, but employs poetic

techniques such as heightened imagery, parataxis, and emotional effects. There is no formal structure or rhyme scheme, and the rhythm is more akin to prose than traditional poetry.

Notable Works and Creators:
Charles Baudelaire's "Paris Spleen" is considered one of the seminal works of prose poetry. Other notable prose poets include Gertrude Stein, Oscar Wilde, and Allen Ginsberg.

Unique Features:
Prose poetry blurs the line between prose and poetry by employing the ordinary language and structure of prose while incorporating poetic elements like imagery and rhythm. It often focuses on capturing a single mood or impression.

ROUNDEL

Origins and History:
The roundel is a form of lyrical poetry that originated in England in the 19th century and is a variation of the French rondeau.

Structure:
A roundel consists of 11 lines, with a rhyme scheme of ABAR BAB ABAR, where R is a refrain. The refrain is usually a short phrase taken from the first line, and it recurs at the end of the second and final stanzas. The meter is often iambic, and the length of the lines is flexible.

Notable Works and Creators:
Algernon Charles Swinburne is credited with creating the roundel form in English. His poem "The Roundel" is a notable example, and he used the form in many of his poems.

Unique Features:
The roundel is characterized by its use of a refrain and a specific rhyme scheme. It is often used for lyrical and musical expression, and it has a cyclical structure due to the repeated refrain.

SESTINA

Origins and History:
The sestina is a complex poetic form that originated in 12th-century Provence, France. It was developed by the troubadour Arnaut Daniel and later spread throughout Europe. It became popular among Italian and English poets during the Renaissance.

Structure:
A sestina consists of six stanzas of six lines each, followed by a three-line envoi, for a total of 39 lines. The words that end each line of the first stanza are used as line endings in each of the following stanzas, rotated in a set pattern. The envoi uses all six words, two per line. There is no rhyme scheme, but the repetition of the end-words creates a sense of unity and structure.

Notable Works and Creators:
Dante Alighieri and Petrarch are notable early practitioners of the sestina. In English, Elizabeth Bishop's "Sestina" is one of the most famous examples of this

form.

Unique Features:
The sestina is known for its intricate pattern of repeated end-words and its lack of rhyme. It requires a high degree of technical skill to write, and is often used to explore complex emotions or concepts.

SLAM POETRY

Origins and History:
Slam poetry originated in the 1980s in Chicago as a competitive form of performance poetry. It was created by construction worker and poet Marc Smith, who sought to bring poetry back to the audience through energetic performances. Slam poetry has since become a global movement.

Structure:
There is no fixed structure or style for slam poetry. It is defined more by its performance aspect than its written form. Poems can vary in length, style, and subject matter. The emphasis is on the poet's ability to convey emotion and connect with the audience through their performance.

Notable Works and Creators:
Marc Smith is considered the founder of the slam poetry movement. Other notable slam poets include Patricia Smith, Saul Williams, and Taylor Mali.

Unique Features:
Slam poetry is characterized by its energetic and emotive performance style. Poets often engage with social and political themes, and audience interaction is encouraged. Slam poetry competitions, or slams, are events where poets perform their work and are judged by members of the audience.

SONNET

Origins and History:
The sonnet originated in 13th-century Italy and is attributed to the poet Giacomo da Lentini. It became highly popular during the Renaissance and was adopted and adapted by poets across Europe, including William Shakespeare and Petrarch.

Structure:
A sonnet traditionally consists of 14 lines of iambic pentameter, with a specific rhyme scheme. The Italian or Petrarchan sonnet is divided into an octave (eight lines) and a sestet (six lines), with a rhyme scheme of ABBAABBA CDCDCD. The English or Shakespearean sonnet is composed of three quatrains and a final rhymed couplet, with a rhyme scheme of ABABCDCDEFEFGG.

Notable Works and Creators:
Notable sonneteers include Petrarch, William Shakespeare, and John Milton. Shakespeare's Sonnet 18 ("Shall I compare thee to a summer's day?") is one of the most famous sonnets in English literature.

Unique Features:
Sonnets are known for their formal structure and lyrical quality. They often

explore themes of love, beauty, and time, and are characterized by a turn or shift in thought, usually between the octave and sestet in the Petrarchan sonnet or before the final couplet in the Shakespearean sonnet.

TANKA

Origins and History:
Tanka is an ancient form of Japanese poetry that predates the haiku. It has been practiced for over 1,300 years and was originally used to convey romantic or emotional content, often in the context of courtly love.

Structure:
A tanka poem consists of five lines with a syllable pattern of 5-7-5-7-7, totaling 31 syllables. Unlike haiku, tanka often includes personal emotions and themes, and it does not require a seasonal reference.

Notable Works and Creators:
The Man'yōshū, compiled in the 8th century, is one of the oldest collections of tanka poetry. Princess Nukata and Ono no Komachi are among the notable tanka poets of ancient Japan.

Unique Features:
Tanka is characterized by its five-line structure and a focus on lyrical expression of emotion. It has a musical quality and is often used to explore themes of love, nature, and personal reflection.

TAUTOGRAM

Origins and History:
The term "Tautogram" is derived from Greek, meaning "same letter." It is a textual form where each word in the text starts with the same letter. Historically, tautograms were used in poetical forms, and in modern times they have been adapted for various uses, including games.

Structure:
In a tautogram, all words in the text must start with the same letter. There is no fixed syllabic, metric, or rhyme scheme associated with tautograms, and they can be of any length.

Notable Works and Creators:
Tautograms are more of a literary device than a form associated with specific poets. They are popular in word games and as a creative writing exercise.

Unique Features:
Tautograms are both a written and visual phenomenon, where the repetition of the initial letter is apparent. This form can be used for fun and wordplay, and it is visually striking due to the repetition of the initial letter. They are used for stylistic effect and can be found in word games such as the 'Same Letter' category in the U.S. game show Wheel of Fortune.

TERZA RIMA

Origins and History:
Terza rima is an Italian poetic form that was first used by Dante Alighieri in

the 14th century in his epic poem, The Divine Comedy. The form was later adopted by other poets and spread beyond Italy.

Structure:
Terza rima consists of tercets (three-line stanzas) with an interlocking rhyme scheme of ABA BCB CDC, and so on. The poem usually ends with a single line or a couplet that rhymes with the middle line of the last tercet.

Notable Works and Creators:
Dante Alighieri's 'The Divine Comedy' is the most famous work written in terza rima. Other notable poets who have used this form include Geoffrey Chaucer, Percy Bysshe Shelley, and W.H. Auden.

Unique Features:
Terza rima is known for its interlocking rhyme scheme, which creates a sense of continuity and flow. It is often used for longer narrative poems and is well-suited to formal, lyrical expression.

TRICUBES

Origins and History:
Tricubes is a contemporary poetic form invented by the poet Philip Larrea. It is a relatively new form that aims to create a compact structure with a strict limitation on the number of words and lines.

Structure:
A Tricubes poem is comprised of three stanzas, each containing three lines, and each line containing three syllables. The structure is therefore denoted as 3x3x3. There is no specific requirement for rhyme or meter, giving poets freedom to explore a variety of themes and tones within the compact form.

Notable Works and Creators:
Philip Larrea, a poet hailing from California, United States, is credited with the creation of the Tricubes form. Despite being a relatively new poetic form, it has gained recognition in various poetry circles for its simplicity and elegance.

Unique Features:
Tricubes are a popular choice for poets who wish to convey a compact, concise thought, image, or emotion. The form's simplicity lends itself well to exploring a single idea or image, and its compactness encourages economy of language The key feature of Tricubes is its strict syllable count and stanza structure. This form encourages poets to focus on word choice and imagery, given the limited syllable count.

TRIOLET

Origins and History:
The triolet is a poetic form that originated in France in the 13th century. It was initially used for light or humorous content and later evolved to include more serious themes.

Structure:
A triolet consists of eight lines with a rhyme scheme of ABaAabAB. The first,

fourth, and seventh lines are identical, as are the second and eighth lines. This creates a tight structure with repeated lines.

Notable Works and Creators:
Robert Frost's "The Last Word of a Bluebird" and Thomas Hardy's "How Great My Grief" are notable examples of triolets in English literature.

Unique Features:
The triolet is known for its tight structure and repetition. It often has a lyrical, song-like quality due to the repetition of lines, and it is well-suited to expressing a single thought or emotion.

VILLANELLE

Origins and History:
The villanelle is a French verse form that has evolved over time. English has become its natural home. It was originally meant to mimic an Italian villanella, a dance song.

Structure:
The villanelle comprises 19 lines made up of five tercets (three-line stanzas) and a concluding quatrain. It has a complex repeating pattern. The first and third lines of the first stanza are refrains that repeat alternately at the end of other stanzas and then both repeat at the end of the final quatrain.

Notable Works and Creators:
One of the most famous villanelles in English is "Do Not Go Gentle into That Good Night" by Dylan Thomas. Elizabeth Bishop's "One Art" is another notable example.

Unique Features:
The repeating lines of a villanelle make it ideal for exploring a single thought or idea in a deep and complex way. The form is also noted for its musicality and can be used to create a song-like effect.
Eight of the 19 lines are repeated, meaning the poem only needs 13 unique lines. The repetition creates a complex interplay of themes and ideas that can be used to create a deep and nuanced exploration of a single thought or idea.

Bibliography

The bibliography section lists all the sources used in this book, including websites offering in-depth knowledge on varied poetic forms and terminologies. These resources, which contributed significantly to this book's creation, are shared here to invite further exploration into poetry.

Do remember, websites can change or disappear, potentially affecting the availability of referred content. The bibliography is alphabetically arranged for your convenience, though accuracy of the information contained lies with the authors and publishers of the listed sources.

Inspirational Quote:

"He laughs. "What do I smell like?" "Petrichor." "I don't even know what that means." "It's a word that describes the smell of fresh rain after warm weather." "I had no idea there was a word for that." "There's a word for everything."
— Colleen Hoover, **Verity**

References:

Aha! Poetry, *www.ahapoetry.com*
Britannica, *www.britannica.com*
Poets.org, *www.poets.org*
Poets Collective, *www.poetscollective.org*
Poetry Foundation, *www.poetryfoundation.org*
Writer's Digest, *www.writersdigest.com*
Wikipedia, *www.wikipedia.org*

Inspiring Artists:

Aaron Douglas	Charles Dana Gibson	Mark Lague	Elizabeth Catlett	Sandra Chevrier
Erin Hanso		Pascal Campion	Leo and Diane Dillon	Charles Addams
Brian Kesinger	Vincent van Gogh	Leonid Afremov		Audrey Kawasaki
Lois van Baarle	Liam Wong	Robert Crumb	Aleksi Briclot	Norman Rockwell
Harrison Fisher	Eyvind Earle	Patrice Murciano	Ben Templesmith	Gerda Wegener
Guy Denning	Laurie Greasley	Ronald Wimberly	Carne Griffiths	Arthur Rackham
Qi Baishi	Skottie Young	Studio Ghibli	Victo Ngai	

Glossary

This glossary is organized in a unique manner, designed to gradually build your understanding of poetic language and concepts, rather than a simple alphabetical listing. Each term is introduced and explained in a context that extends from the previous definitions, allowing the glossary to not just define terms, but tell a story of how these elements interact and build upon each other in poetry.

Syllables: The basic units of sound that make up words.

Unstressed Syllables: The parts of words that are pronounced with less emphasis.

Stressed Syllables: The parts of words that are emphasized or spoken with more force.

Metrical Feet: Basic units of measurement in poetic meter, such as iamb, trochee, dactyl, and anapest.

Iamb: An iamb is a metrical foot consisting of one unstressed syllable followed by one stressed syllable. This pattern is called iambic.

Trochee: A trochee is a metrical foot consisting of one stressed syllable followed by an unstressed syllable.

Dactyl: A dactyl is a metrical foot consisting of one stressed syllable followed by two unstressed syllables.

Anapest: An anapest is a metrical foot consisting of two unstressed syllables followed by one stressed syllable.

Trimeter: In poetry, trimeter refers to a line of verse consisting of three metrical feet.

Anapestic Trimeter: An anapestic trimeter is a metrical pattern in poetry in which each line consists of three anapests.

Pentameter: Pentameter refers to a line of verse consisting of five metrical feet.

Hexasyllabic: Each line of the poem consists of six syllables.

Octosyllabic: Each line of the poem consists of eight syllables.

Quatrain: A quatrain is a stanza consisting of four lines, often with a specific rhyme scheme like ABAB or AABB.

Couplet: A couplet is two lines of verse that usually rhyme and have the same meter.

Tercet: A tercet is a stanza consisting of three lines. It can have various rhyme

Redondilla: A Spanish poetic form consisting of a quatrain with a rhyme scheme of ABBA.

Rhyme: The correspondence of sounds between words or the endings of words.

Alliteration: The repetition of the initial consonant sounds in adjacent or closely connected words.

Assonance: The repetition of vowel sounds in non-rhyming words that are close to each other.

Consonance: The repetition of consonant sounds, typically at the end of words.

Onomatopoeia: The formation of words that imitate or suggest the natural sounds associated with them.

Simile: A figure of speech that compares two unlike things using "like" or "as."

Metaphor: A figure of speech that compares two unlike things without using "like" or "as."

Personification: The attribution of human qualities to non-human entities.

Imagery: Imagery refers to the use of vivid and descriptive language that creates sensory experiences and appeals to the reader's senses (sight, sound, taste, touch, smell). It helps to create a vivid mental picture and adds depth to the poem.

Symbolism: The use of objects, characters, or actions to represent abstract ideas or qualities.

Irony: The use of language that signifies the opposite of what is expected for emphasis or humor.

Hyperbole: Exaggerated statements or claims not meant to be taken literally.

Oxymoron: The combination of contradictory terms for a dramatic effect.

Repetition: The repeated use of words, sounds, or phrases for emphasis or rhythmic effect.

Refrain: A repeated line or group of lines at regular intervals in a poem., usually at the end of a stanza.

Enjambment: The continuation of a sentence or phrase beyond the end of a line or stanza in poetry.

Caesura: A pause or break in a line of poetry, often near the middle.

Envoi (or Envoy): A short stanza at the end of a poem used to address an imagined or real person or to comment on the preceding body of the poem.

Ayes: An archaic or poetic way of saying "yes" or expressing agreement.

Ebb: The movement of the tide out to sea or a decline or reduction in something.

Anima: *In psychology, especially in Carl Jung's theory, it refers to the inner feminine side of a man. In general, it can also mean the soul or inner self.*

Octave: *An octave is a stanza consisting of eight lines.*

Rhyme Scheme: *The pattern of rhymes at the end of each line in a stanza or poem.*

Kigo: *A term in traditional Japanese poetry, especially haiku, indicating a word or phrase associated with a season.*

Stanza: *A stanza is a group of lines in a poem, often considered a poetic paragraph. It functions as a structural unit within a poem, with a specific pattern of line breaks and often sharing a common theme or thought.*

Verse: *Verse refers to a single line of poetry. It can also refer to a section of a poem that is characterized by a specific rhyme scheme, meter, or form.*

Sestet: *A six-line stanza, or the final six lines of a 14-line Italian or Petrarchan sonnet. A sestet refers only to the final portion of a sonnet, otherwise the six-line stanza is known as a sexain.*

Sexain: *A stanza with six lines that may or may not rhyme (or a sestet if it is the final lines of a sonnet).*

Blank Verse: *Poetry written in unrhymed iambic pentameter.*

Free Verse: *Poetry that does not rhyme or have a regular meter.*

Acknowledgments

This journey, this book, emerged as a personal challenge. A secret endeavor, daring me to immerse myself in every aspect of its creation. From the conceptualization of content, the careful crafting of structure, meticulous editing, to the manifestation of art that graces its pages - it was a solitary pilgrimage of the mind, the heart, and the senses.

Yet, even in this solitude, I was not alone. Inspiration has many faces, and while few have directly contributed to the tangible parts of this creation, there are those whose influence subtly permeated each page, each line, each word.

For my beloved wife, Nicole,

Though the pages of this book bear no direct signature of your hand, they pulse with the rhythm of your influence. Just as the moon quietly moves the tides, so have you shaped the contours of my thoughts, my words, my very soul. You, my muse, have served as the silent compass guiding me through the uncharted seas of creation.

In every line I penned, in each idea that blossomed, I found reflections of you, of our love, our shared dreams and whispered secrets. You are the hidden melody in my prose, the unseen hand that weaves beauty into my words. The phrases may not echo your voice, but they hum with the cadence of your inspiration, our shared laughter, the comforting silence we've grown to cherish.

You are the lifeblood that courses through my work, unseen yet ever-present. Like a precious scent, your essence lingers, a subtle reminder of the love that propels each word, each stroke of ink upon this canvas of dreams.

Your love, the fire in my heart, fuels the brilliance of every dawn I capture in verse. It is in the quiet spaces between words where your influence resides, resonating deeper than any melody, more vibrant than any painted sunset.

So, though your name does not grace the byline, this book - and all I create - is a testament to you. To your love, your light, your indomitable spirit. You are the heart within my artistry, the soul within my words. And for that, and for everything, I dedicate this book to you.

Forever yours, with all my love.

My sincerest gratitude goes to everyone who, knowingly or unknowingly, illuminated this path for me. Though the journey was mine to tread, the footprints of inspiration belong to you.

Born and raised near the runway of an Air Force base in Fairborn, Ohio. Brandon Board found his mind often soaring with the roaring jet engines that were a constant backdrop to his childhood. Today, his feet are firmly planted on the ground, but his thoughts and creativity still take flight, manifesting in a remarkable array of interests, hobbies, and skills.

Brandon's life story unfolds like a kaleidoscope, shifting and transforming with every new hobby, interest, and skill he explores. Each experience, no matter how diverse or unrelated, reflects his enduring thirst for knowledge and determination to go beyond the ordinary. While these pursuits may seem varied to some, they are, to Brandon, merely different shades of his vibrant palette of life.

One such pursuit, borne out of a whiff of nostalgia, was the exploration of the sensory world. The scent of Petrichor, the earthy aroma that fills the air after rain, sparked an unexpected chapter in Brandon's journey – his foray into the world of publishing. Upon discovering that this sensory memory from his childhood had a name, he was propelled into a fascination with the intricate bond between our senses and our emotions.

Petrichor, for Brandon, was more than just a smell; it was a moment frozen in time, a portal to profound reflections. The aftermath of a rain shower, a world bathed in golden glow, a pause in the rhythm of life, it was the universe's invitation to stand still and contemplate. Such is the power of sensory experiences, often unnoticed, yet capable of evoking the deepest of thoughts and emotions.

'Sensory Chronicles - A Poetic Odyssey Through the Five Senses' is the ambitious result of that journey. With the same fervor he brings to his numerous hobbies, Brandon has crafted a series that intertwines poems, illustrations, and sensory experiences in a tapestry of thought, emotion, and perception. His love for the concept, for the intricate puzzle of weaving everything together, shines through every page, making each book more than just a collection of poems - they are experiences in themselves.

Today, Brandon resides just a stone's throw from his hometown, living his best life, ever-curious and ever-ready for the next hobby, the next passion, the next grand idea.

www.ingramcontent.com/pod-product-compliance
Lightning Source LLC
Chambersburg PA
CBRC091210010526
44119CB00019B/366